NOW AND THEN

A guide to preparing for the inevitable *now* rather than repairing *then*

Dr. Norman L. Collins, Sr.

RALEIGH, NORTH CAROLINA

Dr. Norman L. Collins/Rain Publishing, LLC
PO Box 14397
Raleigh, NC 27620
www.rainpublishing.com

Now and Then/ Norman L. Collins, Sr. -- 1st ed.
ISBN 979-8-9855005-3-0

ACKNOWLEDGEMENTS

As with my previous two books, I must take a moment to acknowledge and honor individuals who have greatly impacted my life through encouragement, prayer, mentoring, and simply just being there. I first want to give the highest honor to my Lord and Savior Jesus Christ for the ability to comprehend and express what has been laid on my heart to be a blessing to readers and listeners everywhere. A special thanks and honor to the memory of my late pastor, Rev. Charles M. Johnson, who recognized my love for people and my ability to write and encouraged me to write books that one day would be bestsellers.

My seven children have been and will continue to be a source of my inspiration through their words of encouragement, especially when they utter the words "Daddy, I'm so proud of you." I want to give thanks to special friends Tony Graham who has rendered major support during and after my endeavors, Willie "Deacon" Hale who always encourages me with "Bishop, you got this!", and Frank Leggett whose career in insurance allowed him to educate and update me more on the need for life insurance and other insurances that are important NOW and THEN. A final thanks goes to Rachel Renee Griggs and the Rain Publishing Company for investing their professional services and assistance in my effort to fulfill my desire to develop and publish this NOW and THEN Guide that I believe will positively impact all those who use it.

FOREWORD

"Teach us to realize the brevity of life, so that we may grow in wisdom."
Psalms 90:12

This quote, penned by the patriarch Moses, reminds us to be aware of the fact that the term or the length of our life is brief and uncertain and that we should embrace moments in life as teachable ones so that we can gain wisdom from the events therein.

If there is anything that the Covid pandemic has taught us is that sickness and death are unpredictable, and both are often met with anxiety and frustration by our loved ones who are often placed in a position of "what do we do now?" It has been said in different ways, but it is true – "Life is uncertain, but death is sure." Because life is uncertain, we never know when severe or terminal illness may occur which can render one helpless physically and/or psychologically.

Furthermore, death can occur without any warning through sickness or by other means such as massive heart attacks, accidents, major strokes, aneurisms, or other natural occurrences. Trying to navigate through the business affairs of a loved one due to their being incapacitated through sickness or death can be a major challenge if there is no plan put in place by the loved one before such life-altering events occur. Unfortunately, many are caught unaware of life's uncertainties and have made little or no preparation for them. Plain and simple is the fact that being "proactive" prevents the unwarranted turmoil of being reactive. The famous author and motivational speaker John Maxwell once said, "If you're proactive, you focus on preparing. If you're reactive, you end up focusing on repairing." Whereas we have little to no control over life's uncertainties, we can take the necessary steps to avoid many of the challenges that come with them.

Most people shrug or cringe at speaking or thinking about death, whether it is theirs or that of loved ones. Perhaps you have experienced the challenge of assisting a loved one with medical care but who, due to the severity of their illness, was unable to share medical or family history information that would be useful to their medical attendants in caring for them. Then there's the experience of planning the memorial or funeral service for a loved one who left no instructions regarding their wishes or provided no information regarding life insurance policies, finances, or other business-related matters.

Both scenarios can be overwhelming, and grief is compounded by the lack of knowledge regarding the whereabouts or existence of such information. Furthermore, it is also unfortunate and grievous that chaos and confusion are created among family members who seek to resolve business matters and to bring some sense of mitigation to the grief process. I am reminded of a time when one of my siblings passed away, and even though she acclaimed to have her business affairs in order (i.e., life insurance policy, living will, etc.), our family was unable to find any sign of such documents and were thus left to deal with having to scramble to make funeral preparations which, in addition to the grief, exacerbated our pain.

Therefore, it behooves each of us to meet those challenges of uncertainty by making the necessary preparations NOW rather than THEN! It is for such purpose that NOW and THEN is created as a guide to assist those who struggle with how to NOW to prepare for that moment of when and THEN!

To this end, NOW and THEN Planning Guide" is a tool developed to assist individuals and their families with the challenges of navigating important business matters in an organized manner PRIOR to the major illness and/or death of a loved one. Some of the forms included may not be conducive to your needs. However, at the very least this guide will provide the basic information you can provide NOW that will greatly assist whomever you assign to handle your business affairs THEN.

So that this guide will be most useful, please follow these steps:

1. Complete forms with as much information as possible. It may be necessary to receive assistance from a trusted family member or friend in filling out the forms.

2. Be sure to sign, date, and have notarized the CERTIFICATION OF VALIDITY form located behind the Table of Contents page.

3. Make a copy of the documents in this booklet to either share with your trusted proxy, be it family, friend, attorney, etc. At the very least be sure to store this booklet in a safe place (security box, vault, a bank safe deposit box) and make your proxy aware of its location.

4. Remember to update your documents as needed based on changes in circumstances, such as change of contact info, proxy, location of additional property or sale of property, etc.

5. NOTE: If you are using the online version of this guide, you can update your document, save all documents to a jump drive or other external data storage device and store it in a safe place. As with paper documents, be sure to inform whomever you choose regarding the whereabouts of the external data storage device.

I also HIGHLY suggest and advise that you consider the following actions you can take to prepare NOW for THEN:

1. Obtain life insurance to prevent unwarranted financial duress upon your loved ones
2. Choose a local mortuary/funeral home and obtain pre-arrangement and/or pre-paid funeral plans
3. Obtain a Living Will and Directive to prevent uncertainty and potential chaos among family
4. Communicate with family members or other chosen trusted persons regarding business and medical matters.

CONTENTS

Certification of Validity

This is to certify that

I, _____ being of sound mind and legal capacity, have completed, reviewed, and ascertained that the content included in the following pages of the NOW and THEN Guide are valid and true to the best of my ability and express my desires where applicable.

No modifications are to be made to these documents without my expressed written consent or that of whomever I have assigned as my executor listed below.

Signed this _____ day of _____, 20____

_____   _____
OWNER (printed)   OWNER Signature

_____   _____
WITNESS - Appointed Executor   WITNESS Signature

State of _____
County of _____

I, _____, Notary Public, do hereby certify that _____ personally appeared before me this day and acknowledged the due execution of the foregoing instrument.

Witness my hand and official seal this _____ day of _____, 20___.

_____
Official Signature of Notary
(Official Seal)

_____
Notary's Printed or Typed Name

Notary Public
My Commission Expires: _____

PERSONAL DATA

This section is designed to share information that can be referred to as needed for various circumstances where such information is useful, such as completing applications, vital record retrievals, etc. Of course, as with this and other sections of the guide, some information may or may not be relevant for you.

The Emergency Contact section is extremely necessary in the event that you are unable to provide the information verbally due to illness or death. Being able to contact your physician in the event of an emergency could be a life-saving measure. In addition, if you do not have a primary or family physician, now may be the time to secure one for the sake of medical history records that can be located by one medical facility as opposed to several.

Veteran Data is helpful in the event that veteran social and medical services are needed as well as to be included in family and ancestral records. It is also useful by families and mortuaries when planning funeral or memorial services

Education, Academic Honors/Awards, and Club/Fraternity/Sorority/Lodge Memberships sections are useful for biographical development, family record-keeping, and of course for the creation of obituaries for funeral/memorial services and media announcements.

NOTE: This document does not include the placement of your Social Security number. However, you can either include a copy of your Social Security card in the "Document" section in the rear of this guide OR keep a copy where it can be easily retrieved by whomever you choose to advise of the location of your card and/or this guide.

Personal Data Form

NAME_____
First   Middle   Maiden   Last   Jr Sr/other

ADDRESS_____
Street   City   County   State   Zip Code

PHONE: ❑ Cell _____ ❑ Home _____ ❑ Work _____

EMAILS: _____   _____

DATE OF BIRTH: _____   PLACE OF BIRTH _____

ETHNICITY/RACE

Do you consider yourself to be Hispanic/Latino? ❑Yes ❑ No
In addition, select one or more of the following racial categories to describe yourself:
- ❑ American Indian or Alaska Native
- ❑ Asian
- ❑ Black or African American
- ❑ Native Hawaiian or Pacific Islander
- ❑ White U.S.

WORK AUTHORIZATION

U.S. Citizen/ Resident Alien? _____
If NO, please complete the following:
     Visa Type _____ Years in the U.S. _____

EMPLOYMENT

Current Employer _____
Position(s) _____
Employer Contact _____ Phone Number _____

Former Employers:
_____
_____
_____
_____

MARITAL STATUS: ❑ **Single**   ❑ **Married**   ❑ **Divorced**   ❑ **Widowed**

SPOUSE OR DOMESTIC PARTNER

Name_____
First   Middle   Maiden   Last   Jr Sr other

Address_____
Street   City   County   State   Zip Code

Phone: ❑ Cell _____ ❑ Home _____ ❑ Work _____

Emails: _____   _____

EMERGENCY CONTACT

Name _____
      First   Middle   Maiden   Last   Jr Sr other

Relationship _____

Address _____
      Street   City   County   State   Zip Code

Phone: ☐ Cell _____ ☐ Home _____ ☐ Work _____

Emails: _____   _____

PHYSICIAN

Name _____

Address _____

Phone _____ Email _____

Medications Prescribed _____
_____

VETERAN DATA (If applicable)

Branch of Service   ☐ Army   ☐ Navy   ☐ Air Force   ☐ Marine   ☐ Coast Guard

Rank _____ **Serial number:** _____

Dates Served:
    From _____ To _____

Places _____
_____
_____
_____

War Record _____
_____
_____

Awards/Honors
_____
_____
_____
_____

EDUCATION

	Name	Location	Years Attended	Degree/Certificate
Primary School				
High School				
College				
College				
College				
Other				
Other				

ACADEMIC HONORS / AWARDS

_____
_____
_____
_____

CLUB/FRATERNITY/SORORITY/LODGE MEMBERSHIPS:

Organization Name	Position Held	Date(s)

Comments:

_____
_____
_____
_____
_____
_____

FAMILY HISTORY

This section is of great importance for several reasons. These include but are not limited to:

- It provides a brief snapshot of recent genealogy that can be used for medical history that assists physicians in determining potential diagnosis and treatment of certain illnesses and other medical concerns.
- It provides information that can be used for historical family records for such occasions as family reunions, funerals/memorial services, as well as data for bios.
- It provides contact information in the event of an emergency where family members need to be contacted or simply a directory of family members for your own personal use for things such as birthdays.

Please note that several spaces are provided to include immediate family and others whom you consider family should you, like me, have a large family and/or extended family.

If a family member is deceased, you want to include them in this section but indicate "Deceased" and the date of their death (if known) in either of the sections regarding contact info (i.e. address, phone, email).

Family History Form

FATHER

Name_____
   First   Middle   Last   Jr/Sr other

Address_____
        Street   City   County   State   Zip Code

Phone: □ Cell _____ □ Home _____ □ Work _____

Emails: _____   _____

MOTHER

Name_____
   First   Middle   Maiden   Last   Jr/Sr other

Address_____
        Street   City   County   State   Zip Code

Phone: □ Cell _____ □ Home _____ □ Work _____

Emails: _____   _____

CHILDREN

Name	Relationship	Address	Phone #	Email	Date of Birth

SIBLINGS

Name	Relationship	Address	Phone #	Email	Date of Birth

GRANDCHILDREN

Name	Relationship	Address	Phone #	Email	Date of Birth

ADDITIONAL FAMILY: *Children, grandchildren, siblings, aunts, uncles, nieces, nephews, cousins, special friends, etc.*

Name	Relationship	Address	Phone #	Email	Date of Birth

FINANCIALS

As we may know, aside from personal health, a person's finances are of immense importance and high priority when it comes to emergent situations such as sickness and especially death. As mentioned in the foreword of this guide, trying to locate important documents during times of crisis such as sickness or death can be very stressful for family members and/or caregivers. For this reason, it becomes necessary to take measures NOW to avoid both delays in the provision of much-needed services to you during sickness as well as the compounded grief of family during the death of their loved one THEN.

This section is also helpful to you in maintaining a record of your financials when needing to review them for various financial needs for things like quick access to account and policy numbers and for property modifications and locations.

Again, I reiterate that some or much of the space provided in this section may or may not apply to you. However, I am of the persuasion that it is better to have and not need it NOW than to need it and not have it THEN.

Financials List

Institution / Contact	Address / Phone	Type of Account	Account #	Beneficiary
		□ Checking □ Savings □ Money Market □ IRA □ 401K □ Other		
		□ Checking □ Savings □ Money Market □ IRA □ 401K □ Other		
		□ Checking □ Savings □ Money Market □ IRA □ 401K □ Other		
		□ Checking □ Savings □ Money Market □ IRA □ 401K □ Other		
		□ Checking □ Savings □ Money Market □ IRA □ 401K □ Other		
		□ Checking □ Savings □ Money Market □ IRA □ 401K □ Other		
		□ Checking □ Savings □ Money Market □ IRA □ 401K □ Other		

SAFE DEPOSIT BOX(ES)

Institution	Location	Box / Key Number

IMPORTANT COMMENTS:

_____
_____
_____
_____

15

Other Financials

CREDIT CARDS

Credit Card Company	Account #	Credit Card Limit

OTHER CREDITORS

Creditor	Description of Property	Account #

PROPERTIES

Type of Residence	Location	Mortgage Lien Holder (if applicable)
□ House □ Townhouse □ Condo □ Other		
□ House □ Townhouse □ Condo □ Other		
□ House □ Townhouse □ Condo □ Other		
□ House □ Townhouse □ Condo □ Other		
□ House □ Townhouse □ Condo □ Other		

IMPORTANT COMMENTS:

_____
_____
_____
_____
_____

17

VEHICLES *(Titles in "Document" section)*

Type of Vehicle	Year / Make / Model	Lien Holder (if applicable)
□ Car □ Truck □ SUV □ Motorcycle □ Boat		
□ Car □ Truck □ SUV □ Motorcycle □ Boat		
□ Car □ Truck □ SUV □ Motorcycle □ Boat		
□ Car □ Truck □ SUV □ Motorcycle □ Boat		

INSURANCES *(See policies in "Document" section)*

Type	Insurance Company	Policy Number	Face Value
□ Life / Burial □ Medical □ Homeowner/Rental □ Auto			
□ Life / Burial □ Medical □ Homeowner/Rental □ Auto			
□ Life / Burial □ Medical □ Homeowner/Rental □ Auto			
□ Life / Burial □ Medical □ Homeowner/Rental □ Auto			
□ Life / Burial □ Medical □ Homeowner/Rental □ Auto			
□ Life / Burial □ Medical □ Homeowner/Rental □ Auto			
□ Life / Burial □ Medical □ Homeowner/Rental □ Auto			

FUNERAL PREFERENCES

Okay, I know hardly anyone wants to talk about our THEN, but we must face the fact that one day our journey here on earth will end in death. So why not be prepared for it NOW and relieve your family of the burden of planning THEN what we can plan and take care of NOW. This section gives you the opportunity to let your family know how you desire to be memorialized and remembered. Whereas it is very specific even to whether you desire to be cremated or embalmed or what memories you want to be included in your memorial service – it is in your power NOW to make it known.

You may not want to be as specific and complete each line item, and that's within your right. You may want to sit down with your family member(s), clergy, funeral home director, or close friend and talk about what line items to include that are best suited for you and them. At any rate, this guide gives you something to think about, talk about and execute NOW.

Funeral Preferences Form

FUNERAL HOME ASSIGNMENT:

Name _____

Address _____
     Street   City   County   State   Zip Code

Contact _____

Phone_____ Email _____

Desired method of remain disposal: ☐ Embalming ☐ Cremation

PREFERRED PLACE OF FUNERAL/MEMORIAL SERVICE:

Name _____

Address _____
     Street   City   County   State   Zip Code

Contact _____

Phone_____ Email _____

Officiant _____

Phone_____ Email _____

Scripture Selections / Readings _____

Songs/Music   _____
_____
_____
_____

Flowers   _____

Clothing   _____
_____

Jewelry/Glasses _____

Casket (Wood, copper, bronze, steel)   _____

Open/Closed Casket _____

Pallbearers   _____
_____
_____
_____

Cemetery Name and Telephone _____
_____

Mode of Interment (Burial, Mausoleum, other) _____

Prepaid plot/space number _____

Monument/Tombstone Type _____
Material _____
Inscription _____
_____

Cremation:

Urn (Bronze, wood, marble, other) _____

Disposition of Cremated Remains _____
_____

WHAT I WANT REMEMBERED

Favorite Scriptures, Writings, Music
_____
_____
_____
_____
_____

Hobbies and Interests
_____
_____
_____
_____

Accomplishments
_____
_____
_____
_____

Favorite Memories
_____
_____
_____
_____
_____

Religious Affiliation / Church
_____
_____
_____

IMPORTANT DOCUMENTS

Included in the rear of this guide are pocket folders where, if you choose, you can store important documents that you may need NOW for various reasons, or your family may need THEN. In either case, having these and other documents that may not be mentioned in this guide provide easy access for you and those to whom you entrust access to this guide.

NOTE: You will want to either place these documents in a secured folder along with this guide or if you are using the electronic version of this guide you will want to attach a copy of each document to the guide. As aforementioned, it is crucial that you advise whomever you choose of the location of this NOW and THEN Guide and the documents.

DIGITAL ACCESS

This section is included for those who have one or more Internet/social media accounts that you would permit whomever you entrust access to. You may want to include some pages, such as financial accounts, blogs, or other pages you desire to be accessed upon your inability to access. However, there may be others, such as FaceBook, Instagram, Twitter, and other social media accounts that you may or may not want to be accessed upon your inability to access. Access to anything of yours is totally up to you to decide if it should be accessed at any time by anyone.

Also, you may or may not want to include access to your electronic devices, including your computer, iPad, cell phone, watch, or any other such device. You can include them on this page by listing under "Name of Page" as "Computer" or "Cell phone" or other devices and check the box for "Other." If you need additional space, feel free to make a copy and include it in this section.

Important Documents List

LIVING/LAST WILL AND TESTAMENT

Location

_____

_____

Attorney / Assigned Trustee

_____

_____

Instructions / Comments

_____

_____

SOCIAL SECURITY BENEFITS
Location

_____

_____

Comments

_____

_____

MILITARY RECORDS / VETERAN'S BENEFITS
Location

_____

_____

Comments

_____

_____

DEEDS / MORTGAGES
Location

_____

_____

Comments

_____

_____

AUTOMOBILE TITLES / RECORDS
Location

_____

_____

TAX RETURNS / RECORDS
Location

_____

_____

Comments

_____

_____

Digital Access

NAME OF PAGE	WEBSITE	TYPE	USERNAME	PASSWORD
		☐ Financial ☐ Social Media ☐ Other		
		☐ Financial ☐ Social Media ☐ Other		
		☐ Financial ☐ Social Media ☐ Other		
		☐ Financial ☐ Social Media ☐ Other		
		☐ Financial ☐ Social Media ☐ Other		
		☐ Financial ☐ Social Media ☐ Other		
		☐ Financial ☐ Social Media ☐ Other		
		☐ Financial ☐ Social Media ☐ Other		
		☐ Financial ☐ Social Media ☐ Other		
		☐ Financial ☐ Social Media ☐ Other		
		☐ Financial ☐ Social Media ☐ Other		

Dr. Norman L. Collins, Sr., the owner of H4U2 Consulting LLC, is a father, grandfather, author, pastor, motivational speaker, life coach, and educator who seeks to develop and promote holistic wellness and success to individuals dealing with various life challenges, choices, and circumstances. His wide range of occupational experiences, including being a mental health program administrator, have enabled him to affect positive change in the lives of many. He is a proud member of Phi Beta Sigma Fraternity, Inc.